TRINITY RODMAN
BIOGRAPHY: Rising Star in
Women's Soccer

Sharon D. Avery

Trinity Rodman

• AUTHOR BIOGRAPHY

Sharon D. Avery is a distinguished author and sports journalist with a deep passion for capturing the compelling stories of athletes who shape the world of sports. With a career spanning over two decades, Avery has established herself as a prominent voice in sports literature, known for her insightful and engaging biographies that delve into the lives and careers of influential figures in the sporting world.

Avery's writing career began in journalism, where she honed her skills covering a wide range of sports events and profiles. Her keen interest in the human stories behind the headlines led her to transition into sports biography writing, a field where she has made significant contributions. Her work is characterized by a meticulous research approach and a narrative style that brings out the personal and professional journeys of her subjects.

Throughout her career, Sharon D. Avery has authored several acclaimed biographies, focusing on athletes who have made a significant impact in their respective sports. Her books are celebrated for their depth, accuracy, and ability to connect readers with the triumphs and challenges faced by her subjects. Avery's ability to portray the essence of her subjects, combined with her thorough understanding of the sports world, has earned her a reputation as a leading biographer in the field.

In "Trinity Rodman: Rising Star in Women's Soccer," Avery continues her tradition of delivering compelling and insightful narratives. This biography explores the life and career of Trinity Rodman, a rising star in women's soccer, capturing her journey from a young talent to a prominent figure in the sport. Avery's detailed research and engaging writing style provide readers with an in-depth look at Rodman's achievements, challenges, and impact on women's soccer.

Avery's dedication to her craft is evident in her commitment to telling the stories of athletes with authenticity and respect. Her work not only highlights the accomplishments of her subjects but also sheds light on the broader context of their impact on their sport and society. Through her biographies, Sharon D. Avery aims to inspire and inform readers, offering a window into the lives of those who have achieved greatness in the world of sports.

Sharon D. Avery resides in the United States, where she continues to write and engage with the sports community. Her contributions to sports literature are widely recognized, and she remains an influential figure in the field of sports biography.

• TABLE OF CONTENTS

Trinity Rodman

CONCLUSION

• INTRODUCTION

In the ever-evolving landscape of women's soccer, few names have emerged with as much prominence and excitement as Trinity Rodman. From her electrifying performances on the field to her status as one of the youngest stars in the National Women's Soccer League (NWSL), Trinity Rodman has quickly solidified her place as a powerhouse in the sport. But her journey to stardom is more than just a series of goals and accolades; it's a story of perseverance, determination, and the relentless pursuit of greatness.

Born into a family already acquainted with fame, being the daughter of NBA legend Dennis Rodman, Trinity's path to success wasn't handed to her. Rather, she carved out her own space, building a reputation based on her skill, work ethic, and passion for soccer. Despite the looming shadow of her famous father, Trinity forged her own identity, one that reflects her unwavering commitment to achieving her dreams and her undeniable talent on the pitch.

Trinity Rodman

As a young girl, Trinity's interest in soccer was immediate and consuming. Unlike many children who dabble in multiple sports before choosing a favorite, Trinity's focus was singular from the start. This dedication paid off during her high school years, where she became a standout athlete, catching the attention of coaches and scouts across the nation. Her natural athleticism, combined with her keen sense of strategy on the field, made her a force to be reckoned with at a very young age.

Her transition from high school to Washington State University further showcased her skills. Though her time in college soccer was brief, it was nothing short of remarkable. She quickly made a name for herself as a rising talent, a player capable of changing the game with a single play. Her exceptional performances soon led to her declaring for the NWSL Draft, where she would make history as the youngest player ever to be drafted. Selected second overall by the Washington Spirit, Trinity entered the league with immense expectations on her shoulders.

In her debut season, she proved that she could not only handle the pressure but thrive in it. Trinity's impact on the field was immediate scoring goals, creating opportunities, and displaying a level of maturity beyond her years. Her agility, speed, and ability to read the game made her one of the most exciting players to watch in the league. Trinity Rodman didn't just meet expectations; she exceeded them, earning accolades and praise from teammates, coaches, and fans alike.

But beyond the highlight reels and headlines lies a deeper narrative. Trinity's rise to prominence is also a story of resilience. Growing up with the burden of a famous last name came with its own set of challenges, both on and off the field. Throughout her young life, she has had to navigate the pressures of public scrutiny, balancing her own ambitions with the expectations of those around her. Yet, despite these obstacles, Trinity remained focused on her own journey, determined to be known for her own merits.

As women's soccer continues to grow in popularity worldwide, players like Trinity Rodman are helping to redefine the sport, challenging stereotypes, and pushing the boundaries of what is possible for female athletes. Her journey reflects a new era for women's sports, one where young players are stepping into the spotlight with confidence, passion, and an unshakable belief in their abilities.

Trinity Rodman represents the future of women's soccer, but she also embodies the present, the player to watch, the one who can turn a game around with a single touch. Her story is one of raw talent nurtured by hard work, discipline, and a deep love for the sport. Whether you're a die-hard soccer fan or someone who enjoys stories of perseverance and triumph, Trinity Rodman's journey is an inspiring one.

This biography delves into the life of a young athlete destined for greatness. From her earliest days to her breakthrough moments in the NWSL, we explore the experiences that have shaped Trinity Rodman into the rising star she is today. We take a closer look at her challenges, her victories, and the lessons she's learned along the way. As we follow her path to success, one thing becomes clear: Trinity Rodman's story is far from over. Her potential is limitless, and the future holds even more promise for this incredible young talent.

• CHAPTER 1: EARLY LIFE AND FAMILY INFLUENCE

Trinity Rodman's early life is steeped in both the legacies of sports and the challenges of growing up in a high-profile family. Born on May 20, 2002, in Newport Beach, California, Trinity grew up under the bright lights of fame, not because of her own accomplishments, at least not at first, but because of her famous father, Dennis Rodman. As the daughter of one of the most recognizable basketball players in NBA history, Trinity's childhood was far from ordinary. Dennis Rodman, known for his dominant rebounding skills, flamboyant personality, and multiple NBA championships, cast a long shadow over the Rodman family. However, it was Trinity's mother, Michelle Moyer, who provided the stabilizing force in her life, guiding Trinity and her siblings with strength and determination.

Growing up in the Rodman household was a unique experience for Trinity. While her father's career meant he was often away from home, busy with the demands of professional basketball, Michelle Moyer was the constant figure in her life. Trinity's parents eventually separated, and her relationship with her father became more distant, which added an emotional complexity to her upbringing. Despite the challenges that came with her family situation, Trinity found solace and a sense of purpose in sports. While Dennis Rodman was known for his basketball talents, Trinity gravitated towards soccer at a young age, finding joy and fulfillment in the sport.

From a very early age, it was clear that Trinity was naturally gifted when it came to athletics. Though many assumed she might follow in her father's footsteps by taking up basketball, Trinity forged her own path. Soccer became her passion, and her dedication to the sport was unmistakable. By the time she was in elementary school, Trinity was already making waves in local soccer leagues, displaying a level of talent that far exceeded her age. Her mother, recognizing Trinity's extraordinary potential, provided unwavering support, driving her to games and practices, and ensuring that she had every opportunity to excel.

While some children of famous athletes struggle with the weight of expectation, Trinity embraced the challenges that came with her father's legacy. Rather than allowing herself to be overwhelmed by the attention or comparisons, she channeled her energy into becoming the best soccer player she could be. The drive to succeed came from within, Trinity wasn't content with simply being Dennis Rodman's daughter; she wanted to be known for her own achievements. This determination to carve out her own identity played a significant role in shaping her early years.

Michelle Moyer's influence on Trinity cannot be understated. As a single mother raising her children largely on her own, Michelle embodied resilience and perseverance, qualities that would later be reflected in Trinity's approach to soccer. While Dennis Rodman was often in the public eye for his larger-than-life persona, Michelle was the rock for her children, providing them with the stability they needed. She fostered a sense of independence and self-reliance in Trinity, encouraging her to take ownership of her soccer journey. Under her mother's guidance, Trinity developed not only as an athlete but as an individual who understood the value of hard work, discipline, and mental toughness.

Trinity Rodman

Despite her father's absence for much of her childhood, Trinity remained aware of the impact his career had on her life. She often watched old footage of Dennis Rodman's games, admiring his tenacity and relentless pursuit of excellence on the basketball court. While soccer and basketball are vastly different sports, there was an unmistakable connection between Trinity's style of play and her father's intensity. Just as Dennis was known for his hustle and unrelenting energy, Trinity brought that same mindset to the soccer field. She developed a reputation for never backing down, always pushing herself to be better, faster, and stronger than her opponents.

Trinity's older brother, DJ Rodman, also played a significant role in her early life. DJ pursued a basketball career, playing at Washington State University, and their sibling rivalry pushed Trinity to work even harder. The competitive nature of their relationship was a driving force for Trinity, as she constantly sought to prove herself, not just to her family but to everyone who doubted her ability to step out from her father's shadow. The Rodman family dynamic was one of both support and competition, with each sibling encouraging the other to chase their dreams while pushing themselves to new heights.

As Trinity entered her teenage years, her soccer career began to take off. She joined top-tier youth soccer programs and quickly became a standout player. Coaches took notice of her speed, technical skill, and fierce competitiveness. It wasn't long before Trinity was being scouted by college programs across the country. Despite the attention and accolades, she remained grounded, crediting her mother and the lessons learned from her family for keeping her focused on her goals.

One of the defining moments in Trinity's early life was her decision to forgo college soccer after committing to Washington State University and instead declare for the NWSL draft. While many young players choose to develop their skills in the collegiate system before turning professional, Trinity took a different route, opting to enter the draft as one of the youngest players in NWSL history. Her decision was a testament to her belief in herself and her readiness to compete at the highest level. Though this was a bold move, it showcased the confidence and determination that had been instilled in her from a young age.

Her family's influence extended beyond just her father and brother's sports careers; it also shaped her mindset. Trinity learned early on the importance of resilience, how to persevere through adversity and stay focused on her goals, even when the path was uncertain. While the Rodman name carries with it a legacy of success, it also brought challenges, as Trinity had to navigate the expectations and assumptions that came with being Dennis Rodman's daughter. Yet, instead of shying away from this, she used it as motivation to prove her worth as a soccer player in her own right.

In essence, Trinity Rodman's early life and family influence were marked by a duality of privilege and pressure. Her famous surname opened doors, but it also placed immense expectations on her shoulders. However, rather than allowing these pressures to define her, Trinity embraced them, using her family's legacy as fuel for her own ambitions. Her mother's steady guidance and her father's competitive spirit helped mold her into the player she is today—a rising star in women's soccer, ready to leave her own mark on the sport.

As Trinity continues to make waves in professional soccer, the lessons from her early life remain a driving force in her career. Her family's influence, while complex, has given her a unique perspective on what it means to be successful, not just in sports but in life. Her journey is far from over, but her early years laid the foundation for the incredible accomplishments that were yet to come.

• CHAPTER 2: DISCOVERING THE LOVE FOR SOCCER

Trinity Rodman's love for soccer was not a fleeting interest; it was a passion that seemed to ignite from the very beginning of her childhood. Growing up in a sports-centered family, Trinity was surrounded by athleticism from an early age. However, despite her father Dennis Rodman's deep ties to basketball, she chose a different path, a path that would ultimately define her future and showcase her individual talents. Soccer, unlike basketball, became her world, offering her an outlet to express herself and develop her unique skill set.

In her earliest years, Trinity explored various activities, but it was soccer that captured her heart. There was something about the freedom of the sport, the fast-paced nature, and the constant movement that resonated with her. While many of her peers dabbled in multiple sports or other extracurriculars, Trinity gravitated solely toward soccer. She felt at home on the pitch and found immense joy in every moment spent with the ball at her feet. Soccer wasn't just a pastime for Trinity; it quickly became an obsession.

Her mother, Michelle Moyer, recognized Trinity's early passion and commitment. Unlike some parents who may push their children into sports, Michelle nurtured Trinity's interests organically. She ensured that Trinity had the opportunity to join youth soccer leagues where she could further develop her skills. From a young age, it was clear that Trinity had a special relationship with the sport, one that was driven by an innate passion rather than external pressure.

Trinity's early involvement in local youth leagues allowed her to build a strong foundation in soccer. She excelled quickly, displaying an unusual level of talent for someone her age. Her coaches noticed her exceptional speed, agility, and sense of the game. Even as a young player, she possessed the ability to read the field, anticipate plays, and make smart decisions under pressure. Trinity wasn't just another player on the team; she was often the one making the difference in key moments. Her athleticism was undeniable, but her love for the game was what truly set her apart.

Trinity Rodman

As she progressed through youth soccer, Trinity began to stand out among her peers. It wasn't long before she joined elite soccer clubs, competing against some of the best young players in the country. These experiences only deepened her passion for the sport, as she thrived in environments that pushed her to continuously improve. Trinity enjoyed the challenges, the camaraderie, and the thrill of competition. Every time she stepped onto the field, she felt an overwhelming sense of purpose.

Part of what made soccer so appealing to Trinity was its ability to offer her a sense of autonomy. Unlike her father's basketball legacy, which loomed large over her family, soccer was something Trinity could claim entirely as her own. On the soccer field, she wasn't Dennis Rodman's daughtershe was Trinity Rodman, a talented and determined athlete with a bright future. Soccer gave her the chance to step out of her father's shadow and establish her own identity. The sport became a sanctuary where she could prove her abilities, not just to others, but to herself.

Trinity Rodman

As her talent became more evident, Trinity began to take her training more seriously. She dedicated countless hours to honing her skills, improving her technique, and building her physical strength. While many young athletes might have struggled with balancing schoolwork, social life, and sports, Trinity found a way to stay focused. Soccer was her priority, and she was determined to excel at it. Her work ethic was relentless, and her passion for the game drove her to push past limits that many her age would have found too daunting.

In middle school, Trinity's commitment to soccer took on a new level of intensity. She joined more competitive leagues and began traveling to regional and national tournaments. These experiences not only exposed her to higher levels of play but also allowed her to form relationships with other elite players and coaches. Trinity thrived in this environment, learning from every game, win or lose. The more she played, the more she fell in love with soccer. It was not just about scoring goals or winning trophies; it was about the entire process, the training, the teamwork, the discipline, and the exhilaration of each match.

Trinity Rodman

Despite the growing demands of her soccer career, Trinity always found joy in the sport. She never felt burdened by her commitment to the game. Instead, she embraced every challenge as an opportunity to grow. Trinity's love for soccer was rooted in her genuine appreciation for the game. She loved the strategy involved, the way she could influence the outcome of a match with a well-placed pass or a perfectly timed run. Soccer allowed her to express herself creatively while also providing structure and discipline.

As Trinity transitioned into high school, her soccer journey continued to accelerate. She played for top-tier club teams and quickly became a standout player on her high school team as well. Her reputation as a rising star in youth soccer began to spread, attracting the attention of college coaches and recruiters. Despite her father's fame, it was Trinity's own hard work and dedication that earned her recognition in the soccer community. She was a force to be reckoned with on the field, and her love for the game continued to fuel her drive to succeed.

One of the defining aspects of Trinity's soccer journey was her willingness to go above and beyond what was expected. She never settled for being good enough, she always wanted to be better. Whether it was practicing free kicks until they were flawless or working on her speed and endurance, Trinity was constantly pushing herself to new heights. She understood that talent alone wasn't enough to achieve her dreams; it required effort, perseverance, and an unshakable passion for the sport.

Another key factor in Trinity's soccer development was her ability to learn from others. Throughout her journey, she sought out mentors and coaches who could help her refine her skills and expand her understanding of the game. She was eager to absorb knowledge from those who had more experience, whether it was a club coach, a former professional player, or even her own teammates. Trinity's love for soccer was evident in her curiosity and her desire to always be learning. She knew that to be the best, she had to continue evolving as a player.

Despite her rising profile in the soccer world, Trinity remained humble and grounded. Her love for the game wasn't about fame or accolades, it was about the pure joy she felt every time she stepped onto the field. Soccer gave her a sense of purpose and belonging that she hadn't found in anything else. It allowed her to channel her energy and creativity into something she was truly passionate about. Even as the pressure mounted and expectations grew, Trinity's love for soccer never wavered.

Her passion for soccer also extended beyond just playing the game. Trinity became an advocate for women's sports, using her growing platform to encourage young girls to pursue their athletic dreams. She understood the importance of representation and the need for more female role models in sports. Trinity's love for soccer was not just about her own success; it was about inspiring others to find the same passion and determination that she had discovered.

As Trinity's soccer career continued to flourish, her love for the game remained the driving force behind her success. It was her passion that pushed her to keep improving, her dedication that helped her overcome obstacles, and her love for the sport that fueled her every move on the field. For Trinity Rodman, soccer wasn't just a hobby or a career it was a calling, something that had been a part of her from the very beginning. Her journey was far from over, but one thing was certain: soccer would always be at the heart of who she was.

In discovering her love for soccer, Trinity Rodman found her purpose. It was this love that shaped her as an athlete and as a person, guiding her through challenges and triumphs alike. As she continued to make her mark on the sport, her passion for the game remained as strong as ever, propelling her toward an even brighter future in women's soccer.

• CHAPTER 3: HIGH SCHOOL ACHIEVEMENTS AND CHALLENGES

Trinity Rodman's high school years were a defining period in her soccer journey. During this time, her talent was undeniable, and her ambition to succeed in the sport truly began to take shape. Her high school achievements reflected her commitment and love for the game, yet it wasn't without its challenges. Despite the pressures of balancing academics and athletics, navigating personal expectations, and handling the legacy of her famous father, Trinity pushed through these obstacles with determination and grit. Her high school years showcased not only her incredible talent but also her resilience and ability to overcome adversity.

Trinity attended Corona del Mar High School in Newport Beach, California. From the moment she stepped onto the field for her high school team, it was clear she was a standout player. Her combination of speed, skill, and soccer intelligence allowed her to dominate games, often being the difference-maker for her team. Her natural athleticism, honed by years of hard work and training, gave her an edge over most of her peers. Coaches, teammates, and opponents alike recognized that Trinity was a special player, someone destined for greatness.

One of Trinity's major high school achievements was being named one of the top young soccer players in the nation. She quickly gained recognition as one of the premier talents in high school girls' soccer, which brought her significant attention from college recruiters and professional scouts. Trinity's success was not just due to her raw talent; it was a result of her relentless work ethic. She was constantly training, honing her skills, and improving her game, both on and off the field.

During her time at Corona del Mar High School, Trinity led her team to numerous victories, including deep runs in competitive high school tournaments. Her ability to take control of a game and change the momentum with her decisive plays made her a standout player. Trinity was known for her versatility, being able to excel in various positions on the field. Whether she was scoring goals, setting up teammates, or disrupting the opponent's attack, her presence was felt across every aspect of the game.

Her high school achievements also included earning multiple individual honors and awards. Trinity was consistently named to all-star teams, recognized as one of the best players in her region and across the state. She received several accolades for her performances, including being named league MVP and earning All-CIF (California Interscholastic Federation) honors. These achievements were a testament to her impact on the field, but they were also a reflection of her dedication to the sport.

However, as much as Trinity thrived on the soccer field, her high school years also came with their fair share of challenges. Balancing academics with a rigorous athletic schedule was not an easy task. Trinity was often juggling schoolwork, practice, and travel for games and tournaments. She had to learn how to manage her time effectively to ensure that her academic responsibilities were not neglected while she pursued her soccer dreams. It wasn't always smooth sailing, but Trinity's focus and determination helped her stay on track.

Trinity Rodman

One of the most significant challenges Trinity faced in high school was the weight of expectations. As the daughter of NBA legend Dennis Rodman, she was no stranger to the spotlight. There was an inherent pressure that came with her last name, and many people expected her to excel in sports simply because of her father's legacy. While Trinity was proud of her father's accomplishments, she wanted to make her own mark in the world of sports, and sometimes that meant overcoming the comparisons and assumptions that came with being Dennis Rodman's daughter.

Trinity often had to prove that her success was due to her own hard work and not just the result of her father's fame. This was a challenge that she faced throughout her high school years, as she constantly had to push back against the narrative that her achievements were solely a product of her family's legacy. Trinity used this challenge as motivation, channeling any doubts or criticisms into fuel for her performances on the field. She was determined to carve out her own identity as a soccer player, and she did so with remarkable success.

Trinity Rodman

Another challenge Trinity faced during high school was dealing with the emotional complexities of her family dynamics. Her father's career and public persona often brought attention, both positive and negative, to the Rodman family. Trinity had to navigate the pressures of growing up in the shadow of a celebrity while also managing her personal and athletic goals. Despite these challenges, she remained focused on her soccer career, using the sport as an outlet to escape the difficulties of her family situation.

Trinity also faced challenges from within the competitive world of high school soccer. As one of the top players, she often had a target on her back. Opponents would try to take her out of games by being more aggressive or by focusing their defensive strategies around stopping her. This forced Trinity to constantly adapt her game and find new ways to impact matches. She learned to be resilient, to play through tough situations, and to maintain her composure even when things didn't go her way. These challenges helped her grow as a player and prepared her for the next level of competition.

Trinity Rodman

One of the biggest decisions Trinity had to make during her high school years was about her future in soccer. As she continued to excel, the offers from college programs began pouring in. She eventually committed to play at Washington State University, one of the top soccer programs in the country. This decision was a significant milestone in her high school career, as it marked the next step in her journey toward becoming a professional soccer player. However, it also came with its own set of challenges, as Trinity had to weigh her options and consider what path would be best for her development as an athlete.

Ultimately, Trinity's high school years were defined by both her incredible achievements and the challenges she faced along the way. Her ability to rise above adversity and stay focused on her goals demonstrated her maturity and resilience as both a person and an athlete. Trinity's high school career was a crucial period in her development, laying the foundation for the success that would follow in her professional career.

Through all the ups and downs, Trinity remained committed to her love of soccer. She never let the challenges she faced detract from her passion for the game. In fact, these challenges only strengthened her resolve to succeed. Whether it was the pressure of living up to her family's legacy, the difficulties of balancing school and sports, or the challenges of competing at a high level, Trinity faced everything head-on. She emerged from her high school years as one of the brightest young talents in women's soccer, ready to take on the next chapter of her journey.

Trinity Rodman's high school years were a pivotal time in her life. Her achievements on the soccer field were nothing short of extraordinary, and her ability to overcome challenges set her apart from her peers. Trinity's high school career laid the groundwork for her future success, as she continued to prove that she was more than just the daughter of a famous athleteshe was a rising star in her own right. Her high school experiences, both the triumphs and the trials, shaped her into the player and person she would become, setting the stage for her meteoric rise in the world of women's soccer.

• CHAPTER 4: BREAKTHROUGH AT WASHINGTON STATE UNIVERSITY

Trinity Rodman's time at Washington State University marked a significant turning point in her soccer career, solidifying her status as one of the most promising young talents in the sport. Her breakthrough during this period was the culmination of years of hard work, dedication, and an unwavering passion for the game. At Washington State, Trinity elevated her skills to new heights, honed her mental toughness, and prepared herself for the challenges of competing at the highest level of women's soccer. This chapter of her life was filled with growth, success, and valuable lessons that would shape her journey in the years to come.

Before stepping foot on the Washington State University campus, Trinity had already established herself as a top-tier talent in the world of youth soccer. Her accomplishments in high school and her impressive performances in elite soccer clubs had drawn the attention of numerous college programs. After carefully considering her options, Trinity chose Washington State University, a decision that would set her on a path toward stardom. The program's strong reputation, combined with its emphasis on player development and competitive opportunities, made it the ideal environment for her to continue her soccer journey.

Trinity's freshman year at Washington State was nothing short of remarkable. Even before she had the chance to step onto the field for a regular college season, her potential was evident to both her coaches and teammates. Her arrival generated excitement within the program, and there were high expectations for what she could achieve during her college career. The coaching staff at Washington State recognized her talent and immediately began working with her to refine her skills and prepare her for the rigors of collegiate soccer.

Although the COVID-19 pandemic disrupted the traditional college sports calendar, resulting in the cancellation of the 2020 season, Trinity's time at Washington State still proved to be transformative. Despite not playing a single game for the Cougars, she used the period to train intensely, improve her technical abilities, and gain a deeper understanding of the game. The experience taught her the

Trinity Rodman

importance of patience and perseverance, as she had to navigate the uncertainty of the pandemic while staying focused on her long-term goals.

During this time, Trinity also developed a strong connection with her teammates and coaches, which helped her build a support system that would be crucial for her future success. The culture at Washington State was one of hard work, discipline, and mutual support, which aligned perfectly with Trinity's own values. She embraced the challenges of training in a competitive college environment, pushing herself to be better every day. Her coaches were impressed not only by her talent but also by her dedication and commitment to continuous improvement.

One of the most significant aspects of Trinity's breakthrough at Washington State was her mental development. College soccer, especially at a program as competitive as Washington State, requires players to be mentally tough and resilient. Trinity had to learn how to manage the pressure of expectations, both from herself and from others, and how to stay focused in the face of adversity. These mental skills would prove to be just as important as her physical abilities as she prepared to take the next step in her soccer career.

While Trinity's physical skills were undeniable, her time at Washington State helped her to sharpen her soccer IQ. Under the guidance of experienced coaches, she learned more about the tactical side of the game, positioning, game strategy, and decision-making. Trinity's natural instinct for soccer was refined as she studied different formations, read the flow of the game, and learned how to adapt her style to different situations. This period of growth was instrumental in preparing her for the challenges that would come as she transitioned to professional soccer.

Despite the challenges brought on by the pandemic, Trinity remained undeterred in her pursuit of excellence. She continued to train rigorously, working on her ball control, passing, finishing, and overall fitness. Her relentless drive and determination became even more pronounced during this time. She approached every training session with a mindset of improvement, constantly pushing herself to new limits. Whether she was perfecting her dribbling in tight spaces, working on her shot accuracy, or building her stamina through conditioning drills, Trinity was laser-focused on becoming the best player she could be.

Her time at Washington State was also marked by personal growth. Transitioning from high school to college is a significant step for any young athlete, and Trinity was no exception. She had to adjust to living on her own, managing her academic responsibilities, and maintaining a balance between her studies and soccer. While these changes came with their own set of challenges, Trinity approached them with the same determination she brought to the soccer field. She learned how to navigate the demands of college life while staying focused on her athletic goals.

Washington State University provided Trinity with the opportunity to grow not only as a soccer player but also as a person. She developed strong relationships with her coaches and teammates, who became like family to her. The bonds she formed with her teammates were built on mutual respect and a shared commitment to success. These relationships helped Trinity stay grounded and focused during challenging times, giving her the support she needed to continue pushing forward.

As the pandemic began to ease and opportunities to play soccer returned, Trinity's breakthrough moment arrived. Although she had never played a collegiate game, her talent and potential had not gone unnoticed. Her performances in youth soccer and elite club competitions had already captured the attention of professional scouts. Trinity's decision to declare for the 2021 NWSL Draft marked the next phase of her career, and it was a bold move that demonstrated her confidence in her abilities.

In the 2021 NWSL Draft, Trinity Rodman made history. She was selected as the second overall pick by the Washington Spirit, becoming the youngest player ever drafted into the National Women's Soccer League. This moment was the culmination of all the hard work and dedication she had put in over the years, both at Washington State and throughout her soccer journey. It was also a testament to her immense talent and potential, as professional teams recognized her as a game-changing player who could make an immediate impact in the league.

Trinity Rodman

Trinity's selection in the NWSL Draft was a defining moment, but it was also just the beginning of her professional career. Her time at Washington State had prepared her for this leap into the professional ranks, giving her the tools she needed to succeed at the highest level of women's soccer. The skills she developed, both on and off the field, positioned her for success as she embarked on the next chapter of her journey.

The lessons Trinity learned at Washington State would continue to guide her as she entered the professional world. She carried with her the knowledge that success is not just about talent—it's about hard work, discipline, and the ability to overcome challenges. Her breakthrough at Washington State University was not just about reaching a new level in her soccer career; it was about learning how to handle adversity, stay focused on her goals, and continue striving for greatness.

In her time at Washington State, Trinity Rodman laid the foundation for what would become a remarkable professional career. The skills she developed, the relationships she built, and the experiences she had during this period were instrumental in shaping her as a player and as a person. Washington State was a place of growth, opportunity, and breakthrough for Trinity, setting the stage for her to rise to the top of the women's soccer world.

Trinity Rodman's breakthrough at Washington State University was a pivotal moment in her soccer journey. It was during this time that she truly began to realize her potential as a player and set herself on the path to professional success. Through hard work, dedication, and resilience, she overcame the challenges she faced and emerged as one of the most exciting young talents in women's soccer. Her time at Washington State not only prepared her for the professional ranks but also shaped her into the person she would become, driven by a love for the game and an unwavering commitment to excellence.

• CHAPTER 5: MAKING WAVES IN THE NWSL DRAFT

Trinity Rodman's entry into the National Women's Soccer League (NWSL) through the 2021 NWSL Draft was nothing short of historic. Though she had never played a single game in college, her incredible performances at the youth level had positioned her as one of the most exciting prospects in women's soccer. Her selection in the draft not only set the stage for her professional career but also marked a significant milestone in her journey, highlighting her talent, potential, and dedication to the sport.

Trinity's path to the NWSL Draft was unconventional but remarkable. Most players enter the professional ranks after several years of collegiate play, using college soccer as a stepping stone to build their resumes and gain experience. However, due to the disruptions caused by the COVID-19 pandemic, Trinity's college soccer debut was delayed. She had committed to Washington State University, a prominent program known for developing top-tier talent, but the pandemic forced the cancellation of the 2020 season. Despite not having a collegiate track record, her undeniable skill and promise had already garnered significant attention.

As a player who had already proven her mettle at the youth national level, Trinity's decision to declare for the NWSL Draft was bold but understandable. Having excelled in U.S. youth national teams and showcased her abilities in elite youth competitions, she was ready to take the next step in her career. Her impressive performances in these youth circuits had caught the eye of NWSL scouts, making her one of the most coveted players entering the draft.

The NWSL Draft is a crucial event for women's soccer in the United States, where top college players and young prospects are selected by professional teams. It serves as a gateway for young talents to enter the league and begin their professional careers. The 2021 NWSL Draft was held virtually due to the ongoing pandemic, but the excitement surrounding it was palpable, especially with Trinity's name at the forefront of many conversations.

Trinity Rodman

When draft day arrived, all eyes were on Trinity Rodman. Despite the uncertainty surrounding her lack of collegiate experience, she was highly regarded for her explosive speed, sharp instincts, and technical skills. The buzz around her potential made her one of the top contenders in the draft. And when the Washington Spirit used their second overall pick to select Trinity, she made history as the youngest player ever drafted into the NWSL.

Her selection in the second spot of the draft was a groundbreaking moment. It not only underscored her immense talent but also signified the confidence that the Washington Spirit had in her ability to contribute immediately at the professional level. The Spirit's coaching staff saw in Trinity a rare combination of physical ability, tactical understanding, and raw potential that they believed would translate to success in the NWSL.

The decision to draft a player without college experience, especially so early in the draft, was a bold move by the Washington Spirit. It demonstrated their belief in the trajectory of her career and their desire to invest in a player who had already shown tremendous potential on the youth national stage.

Trinity Rodman

For Trinity, this was a moment of validation, proving that her hard work and dedication to the sport had paid off. She had successfully bypassed the traditional college route to the pros, an achievement few players in women's soccer have managed to accomplish.

While being drafted as the second overall pick was a significant achievement, it also came with enormous expectations. Trinity was stepping into a league filled with seasoned professionals, many of whom had years of college experience under their belts. The pressure to perform and prove herself was immense, but Trinity was unfazed by the challenge. Instead, she embraced the opportunity with the same tenacity and determination that had defined her journey thus far.

Joining the Washington Spirit, Trinity entered a team that was looking to rebuild and strengthen its squad. The Spirit had not been among the top teams in the league in recent seasons, and they were hoping to bring in young talent to help turn things around. Trinity's arrival brought a renewed sense of excitement and optimism to the team. Her energy, youthful exuberance, and willingness to learn made her a perfect fit for a squad that was seeking to establish itself as a contender in the NWSL.

In her first season with the Spirit, Trinity wasted no time making an impact. Despite her youth and lack of collegiate experience, she quickly adapted to the speed and physicality of the professional game. Her versatility allowed her to contribute in various attacking positions, whether as a winger or forward, and she became known for her ability to take on defenders and create scoring opportunities. Trinity's dynamic playing style, characterized by her explosive pace and technical skill, made her a constant threat in the attacking third of the field.

One of the highlights of Trinity's rookie season was her debut performance. In her very first game as a professional, she announced her arrival on the NWSL stage with a goal, showcasing the confidence and poise that had made her a standout prospect. The goal was a statement, Trinity Rodman had arrived, and she was ready to take the league by storm. Her debut not only solidified her place in the starting lineup but also garnered attention across the league, with many recognizing her as a player to watch.

Throughout her rookie season, Trinity continued to make waves. She became one of the most talked-about players in the NWSL, earning praise from fans, coaches, and analysts alike for her performances on the field. Her ability to read the game, combined with her natural athleticism, allowed her to excel in various situations. Whether it was scoring crucial goals, providing assists, or tracking back to help defensively, Trinity proved that she was more than capable of competing at the professional level.

Her breakthrough season with the Washington Spirit was also marked by her ability to rise to the occasion in important matches. In high-pressure situations, Trinity demonstrated maturity beyond her years, delivering clutch performances when her team needed her the most. Her impact was not just limited to her goal-scoring abilities she was also a key playmaker, creating opportunities for her teammates and helping to elevate the overall level of play for the Spirit.

Trinity's success in her rookie season did not go unnoticed. By the end of the year, she had earned numerous accolades, including being named the NWSL Rookie of the Year. This award was a testament to her outstanding performances and her ability to make an immediate impact in the league. Trinity's rookie season had exceeded all expectations, and she had firmly established herself as one of the brightest young stars in women's soccer.

Beyond her individual achievements, Trinity's presence had a transformative effect on the Washington Spirit. With her help, the team made significant strides and became more competitive in the league. Trinity's contributions played a crucial role in the Spirit's journey to the NWSL Championship, a remarkable accomplishment for a team that had been rebuilding. The Spirit's championship victory capped off an extraordinary season, and Trinity's role in their success further cemented her status as a rising star in the sport.

Off the field, Trinity's rise to stardom also brought increased attention to the NWSL and women's soccer in general. As the daughter of NBA legend Dennis Rodman, she was no stranger to the spotlight, but she quickly established her own identity as a professional athlete. Trinity embraced her growing platform, using it to advocate for women's sports and to inspire the next generation of soccer players. Her success became a symbol of what is possible for young female athletes, showing that with hard work and determination, they too can achieve greatness.

Trinity Rodman's breakthrough in the 2021 NWSL Draft was a defining moment in her soccer career. Her selection as the second overall pick, despite her unconventional path to the professional ranks, marked the beginning of a new chapter in her journey. Trinity's rookie season with the Washington Spirit proved that she was more than ready for the challenges of professional soccer, as she delivered standout performances and helped lead her team to an NWSL Championship. Her rise to prominence in the NWSL not only showcased her immense talent but also highlighted her potential to become one of the biggest stars in women's soccer.

• CHAPTER 6: PROFESSIONAL DEBUT AND RISING STARDOM

Trinity Rodman's professional debut marked the beginning of an extraordinary journey in the National Women's Soccer League (NWSL), a moment that would be remembered as a key turning point in her life. Despite the immense expectations placed upon her shoulders, Trinity's first season with the Washington Spirit saw her rise above the pressure and establish herself as one of the brightest stars in women's soccer.

Coming off the excitement of being the second overall pick in the 2021 NWSL Draft, Trinity faced significant scrutiny. As the daughter of NBA legend Dennis Rodman, the spotlight was already intense, but she quickly distanced herself from her father's shadow by creating her own narrative through her passion, commitment, and exceptional performances on the soccer field. Trinity had long shown potential, but stepping into the professional arena would be the true test of her ability to meet the expectations that surrounded her.

Trinity Rodman

The anticipation surrounding Trinity's professional debut was palpable. Fans, analysts, and teammates alike were eager to see how the young forward would handle the pressure of her first professional game. As it turned out, she exceeded even the loftiest of expectations. Trinity's debut came in April 2021 when the Washington Spirit faced the North Carolina Courage in the NWSL Challenge Cup. Despite being a rookie, her performance in that game instantly made her the subject of widespread praise and excitement.

Trinity didn't take long to make an impression. In the 60th minute of her debut match, she scored a stunning goal, showing incredible poise and clinical finishing. Her calmness in front of the goal was remarkable for someone so new to the professional scene. This debut goal not only demonstrated her talent but also signaled her readiness to take on the challenges of professional soccer. The goal stood as a statement to the league: Trinity Rodman was a force to be reckoned with.

As her first season progressed, Trinity continued to build on her strong debut. Her technical skills, combined with her exceptional athleticism, allowed her to stand out in an intensely competitive league. One of her most notable attributes was her ability to take on defenders with confidence, using her speed and agility to create space for herself and her teammates. She had an innate sense of timing and positioning that allowed her to be a constant threat in the attacking third of the pitch.

One key factor that contributed to Trinity's rise in the NWSL was her ability to adapt quickly to the physicality and pace of the professional game. The transition from youth or college soccer to the professional level can be daunting for many players, but Trinity embraced the challenge head-on. Despite being one of the youngest players in the league, she showed no fear when facing more experienced and seasoned opponents. Her resilience and tenacity became defining characteristics of her game, endearing her to fans and earning her respect from her peers.

Throughout the season, Trinity was also a crucial playmaker for the Spirit. Beyond her goal-scoring ability, she developed a knack for creating opportunities for her teammates. Her vision and awareness on the field allowed her to deliver precise passes, and her ability to read the game often put her in positions to set up assists. This playmaking aspect of her game made her a more complete player, proving that she could contribute not only by scoring goals but also by making those around her better.

Trinity's breakout season with the Spirit was further highlighted by her consistent performances in key matches. Whether in regular-season games or the playoffs, she showed an ability to rise to the occasion when it mattered most. Her hunger for success and her drive to win fueled her performances, and she often came through in clutch situations, helping to propel the Spirit to victories when they needed them most.

One of the high points of Trinity's rookie season came during the 2021 NWSL Playoffs. The Washington Spirit had experienced their fair share of challenges during the season, but they entered the playoffs as one of the dark horses in the league. Trinity's performances during the playoffs solidified her reputation as one of the league's top young talents. Her relentless work rate, determination, and skill helped lead the Spirit to the NWSL Championship match.

The 2021 NWSL Championship game was a defining moment for Trinity and the Washington Spirit. Facing the Chicago Red Stars, the Spirit battled through a hard-fought contest that eventually went into extra time. Trinity played a pivotal role in the Spirit's success, constantly pressuring the Red Stars' defense and creating chances for her team. The Spirit ultimately emerged victorious, capturing the NWSL Championship, and Trinity's contributions throughout the playoffs were instrumental in securing the title. It was a dream come true for Trinity, and it solidified her place as a rising star in the sport.

Following the championship win, Trinity's stellar rookie season earned her numerous accolades and recognition. Most notably, she was named the NWSL Rookie of the Year, a prestigious honor that recognized her outstanding contributions during her first season in the league. This award was a testament to her talent, hard work, and determination to succeed at the highest level. Trinity's success during her rookie season had surpassed all expectations, and her future in the league looked incredibly bright.

Trinity's rapid ascent in the NWSL also helped shine a spotlight on the growing popularity of women's soccer. Her rise coincided with a broader movement to elevate women's sports, and her performances contributed to increasing interest in the NWSL. Trinity became a fan favorite, and her dynamic playing style drew attention not only from dedicated soccer fans but also from casual viewers. Her success brought new visibility to the league and helped inspire a new generation of young girls dreaming of following in her footsteps.

Off the field, Trinity's growing stardom also presented new opportunities. As her profile rose, she began to attract attention from sponsors and media outlets eager to feature her as one of the new faces of women's soccer. Trinity embraced these opportunities while remaining focused on her primary goal: continuing to improve as a player and helping her team succeed. She handled the newfound attention with maturity, balancing the demands of her rising fame with her commitment to the game she loved.

Trinity Rodman

One of the reasons for Trinity's rapid success was the support system she had in place. Her family, teammates, and coaches all played important roles in helping her adjust to life as a professional athlete. Despite the pressure, she remained grounded, drawing strength from those around her. Trinity's relationship with her family, particularly her father Dennis Rodman, was often in the spotlight, but she made it clear that her journey was her own. While she appreciated the advice and support from her father, she was determined to carve out her own legacy in soccer.

As Trinity's career progressed, she also became an advocate for women's soccer and women's sports more broadly. She recognized the importance of using her platform to inspire others and to push for greater visibility and equality in sports. Trinity's rise to stardom was about more than just her own successit was also about paving the way for future generations of female athletes.

Trinity Rodman's professional debut and her subsequent rise to stardom in the NWSL were remarkable achievements that showcased her exceptional talent, work ethic, and resilience. Her performances during her rookie season set her apart as one of the brightest young talents in women's soccer, and her impact on the Washington Spirit's NWSL Championship victory cemented her place as a rising star in the sport. As she continued to develop and grow, Trinity's journey was a testament to the power of determination, and her story inspired countless others to pursue their dreams with the same passion and commitment that had driven her to success.

● CHAPTER 7: FACING CHALLENGES AND OVERCOMING ADVERSITY

Trinity Rodman's path to success was far from easy, as she faced numerous obstacles along the way. Like many elite athletes, her journey was defined not just by her moments of triumph but also by her ability to confront and overcome adversity. Despite her undeniable talent, Trinity's rise to stardom came with its own unique set of challenges, both personal and professional, that tested her resilience and determination.

One of the most significant challenges Trinity faced was growing up in the shadow of her father, Dennis Rodman, a legendary figure in basketball known as much for his off-court controversies as for his on-court achievements. While Dennis Rodman's fame brought attention to his daughter's athletic pursuits, it also placed an enormous amount of pressure on Trinity to carve out her own identity. Many observers questioned whether she could live up to her father's legacy or if she was simply benefiting from his fame. Trinity, however, was determined to prove that her success was earned through her own hard work and dedication, rather than a product of her family name.

This dynamic often created added pressure for Trinity as she navigated her early years in soccer. From a young age, she was constantly reminded of her father's fame, and many wondered whether she would pursue basketball or a sport more closely aligned with his legacy. However, Trinity had no intention of following in her father's footsteps. Her passion for soccer was undeniable, and she was determined to make her own mark on the world. The pressure to live up to her family name was intense, but Trinity learned to block out the noise and focus on her own goals.

The absence of a strong, consistent relationship with her father was another personal challenge for Trinity. Dennis Rodman's public struggles with addiction and personal issues created a complicated family dynamic, and his inconsistent presence in her life left Trinity grappling with the difficulties of growing up without a father figure who could offer guidance and support. While Dennis Rodman was famous and celebrated by many, Trinity's relationship with him was strained, which had a profound impact on her during her formative years.

Despite this, Trinity displayed an incredible level of maturity in handling the complexities of her family life. She often spoke about how her father's struggles had given her a deeper understanding of resilience and independence. While she valued the moments she did have with him, she also knew that her journey was hers to navigate on her own. Rather than letting her family circumstances define her, Trinity used them as motivation to create her own path to success.

On the professional front, Trinity also faced numerous challenges. One of the most daunting aspects of her early career was the transition from amateur to professional soccer. The jump from youth or college-level soccer to the National Women's Soccer League (NWSL) is significant, and many players struggle to adapt to the speed, physicality, and demands of the professional game. For Trinity, the transition was made even more difficult by the added pressure of being one of the youngest players in the league and the daughter of a sports icon.

Trinity Rodman

Trinity's rookie season in the NWSL was filled with moments of self-doubt and uncertainty. As she faced off against older, more experienced players, there were times when she questioned whether she belonged at the professional level. The mental and emotional strain of constantly having to prove herself weighed heavily on her, especially as she dealt with the inevitable ups and downs of a professional season. There were matches where things didn't go her way, where she missed scoring opportunities or made mistakes that cost her team. These setbacks were difficult to cope with, but they were also crucial learning experiences that helped Trinity grow as a player.

Injuries were another significant hurdle that Trinity had to overcome. Like all athletes, she faced the risk of physical injury that could derail her progress. During her time with the Washington Spirit, she suffered a few injuries that kept her sidelined for portions of the season. For a young player eager to prove herself, being injured and unable to play was incredibly frustrating. However, Trinity used these periods of recovery to work on her mental game, focusing on her resilience and determination. She learned to listen to her body and prioritize her long-term health, understanding that patience was key to achieving lasting success.

Off the field, Trinity also faced the challenges that come with being a rising public figure. As her profile grew, so did the scrutiny from the media and fans. Every move she made, both on and off the pitch, was analyzed and critiqued, sometimes unfairly. Being in the public eye meant dealing with harsh criticism, especially when things didn't go according to plan. There were times when negative comments from social media or the press would shake her confidence, but Trinity learned to develop a thick skin and focus on what truly mattered, her performance and her growth as a player.

Balancing the demands of a professional career with her personal life was another area where Trinity had to navigate adversity. The grueling schedule of a professional soccer player, with its constant travel, training, and matches, left little time for relaxation or personal pursuits. Trinity had to learn how to manage her time effectively and maintain her mental and emotional well-being amidst the chaos of professional sports. She developed strategies for coping with stress, including focusing on her hobbies outside of soccer and maintaining a strong support system of family and friends.

One of the most significant lessons Trinity learned in overcoming adversity was the importance of mental toughness. Throughout her career, she worked closely with coaches, mentors, and sports psychologists to strengthen her mental game. She realized that success in professional soccer wasn't just about physical ability, it was also about having the right mindset. Developing mental resilience allowed her to stay focused during difficult moments, bounce back from setbacks, and remain confident in her abilities even when things weren't going her way.

As a young woman of color in a predominantly white sport, Trinity also had to confront issues of race and representation. The lack of diversity in women's soccer presented its own set of challenges, and Trinity often found herself navigating spaces where she was one of the few players of color. She recognized the importance of her presence in the sport, not just as a talented player but as a role model for young girls from diverse backgrounds who might not see themselves represented in professional soccer. Trinity used her platform to advocate for greater diversity and inclusion in the sport, knowing that her success could inspire others to pursue their dreams regardless of the obstacles they might face.

Ultimately, the challenges Trinity Rodman faced and overcame played a significant role in shaping her into the player and person she is today. Her ability to rise above the expectations placed on her because of her father's fame, her perseverance in dealing with injuries and setbacks, and her mental toughness in the face of pressure have all contributed to her success. Trinity's journey is a testament to the power of resilience, and her story serves as an inspiration to anyone facing their own struggles.

In the face of adversity, Trinity consistently displayed strength, determination, and an unwavering belief in herself. These qualities, combined with her natural talent and hard work, have allowed her to achieve incredible success at such a young age. Her story proves that overcoming challenges is an integral part of any journey to greatness and that it is often through adversity that true champions are made.

• CHAPTER 8: MAJOR ACHIEVEMENTS ON THE FIELD

Trinity Rodman's career has been marked by a series of remarkable achievements that underscore her exceptional talent and dedication to soccer. From her early days as a rising star to her current status as one of the top players in the National Women's Soccer League (NWSL), Trinity's on-field accomplishments are a testament to her skill, perseverance, and impact on the sport.

One of the significant milestones in Trinity's career came during her rookie season with the Washington Spirit in the NWSL. Drafted as the second overall pick in the 2021 NWSL Draft, Trinity entered the league with high expectations. Her debut season was a showcase of her remarkable abilities, as she quickly became one of the standout players. Trinity's impact was immediate, and she earned widespread acclaim for her performances throughout the season.

A major highlight of Trinity's rookie year was her recognition as the NWSL Rookie of the Year. This prestigious award was given to the most outstanding first-year player in the league, and Trinity's stellar performances made her a clear choice. Her ability to make an immediate impact on the field, combined with her impressive statistics and contributions to the team, solidified her status as a rising star. The Rookie of the Year award was a significant achievement that marked the beginning of what promised to be a stellar career.

Trinity's rookie season was not only marked by individual accolades but also by team success. Her contributions were instrumental in the Washington Spirit's journey to the NWSL Championship. The team faced various challenges throughout the season, but Trinity's performances in crucial matches helped propel them to the top. Her ability to score critical goals and create opportunities for her teammates was a key factor in the Spirit's success. The culmination of their efforts was a well-deserved championship victory, and Trinity's role in the team's triumph was a testament to her skill and influence on the field.

One of the most memorable moments in Trinity's career came during the 2021 NWSL Championship match. Facing the Chicago Red Stars, the Washington Spirit played a fiercely contested game that extended into extra time. Trinity's contributions throughout the match were exceptional, as she showcased her ability to perform under pressure. Her dynamic play and relentless effort were vital in securing the championship, and her performance in this high-stakes game solidified her reputation as a clutch player.

As Trinity continued to develop and mature as a player, her achievements extended beyond her rookie season. She quickly became known for her versatility and adaptability on the field. Trinity's ability to play multiple positions and contribute in various ways made her an invaluable asset to the Washington Spirit. Her technical skills, combined with her physical attributes, allowed her to excel both as a forward and as a midfielder. This versatility not only enhanced her value to the team but also demonstrated her well-rounded abilities as a soccer player.

Another significant achievement in Trinity's career came with her selection to the U.S. Women's National Team (USWNT). Her exceptional performances in the NWSL earned her a spot on the national team, and she made her debut for the USWNT in 2021. Being called up to represent her country was a significant milestone and a recognition of her talent on a global stage. Trinity's inclusion in the national team provided her with the opportunity to compete in international tournaments and showcase her skills against some of the best players in the world.

Trinity's impact on the international stage was further highlighted by her participation in major tournaments, such as the SheBelieves Cup and the Olympic Games. Her performances in these competitions demonstrated her ability to perform at the highest level and contribute to her team's success. Trinity's skill, work ethic, and determination were evident in her play, and she became a key player for the USWNT in various international fixtures.

One of the hallmarks of Trinity's career has been her consistent goal-scoring ability. Her knack for finding the back of the net has been a defining feature of her game, and she has established herself as one of the top goal-scorers in the NWSL. Trinity's goal-scoring prowess has not only contributed to her team's success but has also earned her recognition as one of the premier attacking players in the league.

In addition to her goal-scoring achievements, Trinity's contributions in terms of assists and playmaking have been noteworthy. Her ability to create scoring opportunities for her teammates and deliver precise passes has made her a valuable playmaker. Trinity's vision and creativity on the field allow her to unlock opposing defenses and set up scoring chances, further enhancing her value to her team.

Throughout her career, Trinity has also been recognized for her sportsmanship and leadership qualities. Her dedication to the game and her positive attitude have earned her respect from coaches, teammates, and opponents alike. Trinity's leadership on and off the field has been a source of inspiration for those around her, and her commitment to excellence has set a high standard for herself and her peers.

Trinity's achievements extend beyond individual accolades and team success. Her impact on the sport has been felt in various ways, including her contributions to the growth and popularity of women's soccer. As one of the top young talents in the game, Trinity has helped draw attention to the NWSL and women's soccer as a whole. Her performances and success have contributed to increasing visibility for the sport and inspiring a new generation of players.

Another notable achievement in Trinity's career has been her ability to overcome adversity and bounce back from setbacks. Whether dealing with injuries, personal challenges, or the pressure of high expectations, Trinity has shown resilience and determination in her pursuit of success. Her ability to navigate obstacles and maintain a high level of performance has been a testament to her character and commitment to the game.

Trinity Rodman's career has been marked by a series of major achievements that reflect her exceptional talent and dedication to soccer. From her impressive rookie season and the NWSL Championship to her success with the USWNT and her impact on the sport, Trinity's accomplishments have solidified her status as one of the top players in women's soccer.

Trinity Rodman

Her goal-scoring ability, playmaking skills, and leadership qualities have made her a standout player and a source of inspiration for fans and aspiring athletes alike. Trinity's achievements on the field are a testament to her hard work, determination, and passion for the game, and her continued success promises even greater accomplishments in the future.

• CHAPTER 9: DEVELOPING HER STYLE AND SKILLS

Trinity Rodman's evolution into one of the most exciting talents in women's soccer has been defined by her ongoing development of both style and skills. Her journey from a promising young player to a standout professional involves a meticulous process of honing her craft, understanding the game, and continually pushing her boundaries. This section explores the factors that contributed to her distinctive playing style and how she refined her skills to become a leading force on the field.

From an early age, Trinity displayed a natural aptitude for soccer. Her early experiences in youth leagues and high school competitions provided a foundation for her development, but it was her commitment to improvement and her willingness to embrace various training methods that truly set her apart. One of the key aspects of her development was her focus on building a versatile skill set. Trinity understood that to excel at the highest level, she needed to be adept in multiple facets of the game, including dribbling, passing, shooting, and tactical awareness.

Trinity's dribbling skills, in particular, became one of her standout attributes. She worked tirelessly on her ball control and maneuverability, which allowed her to navigate tight spaces and challenge defenders effectively. Her agility and quick footwork became hallmarks of her style, enabling her to execute intricate moves and create opportunities in high-pressure situations. Trinity's ability to change direction swiftly and maintain close control of the ball made her a constant threat to opposing defenses.

In addition to her dribbling, Trinity placed significant emphasis on her passing accuracy and vision. Recognizing the importance of creating scoring chances for her teammates, she developed a keen sense of where her players were positioned and how to deliver precise passes. Her ability to spot openings and deliver well-timed through balls or cross-field passes allowed her to contribute significantly to her team's attacking play. Trinity's passing skills evolved through countless hours of practice and game experience, and she became known for her ability to make decisive contributions in key moments.

Shooting was another area where Trinity focused on improvement. She understood that being a proficient goal scorer required more than just natural talent, it required technical skill and practice. Trinity honed her shooting technique by working on her accuracy and power. She practiced different types of shots, from long-range efforts to precise finishes inside the box. Her commitment to improving her shooting skills paid off, as she developed a reputation for scoring goals from various positions on the field.

Tactical understanding was also a crucial element of Trinity's development. As she progressed through her career, she worked closely with coaches to gain a deeper understanding of game tactics and strategies. Trinity learned how to read the game, anticipate opponents' moves, and adjust her positioning based on the flow of the match. Her ability to adapt to different styles of play and understand her role within various tactical systems contributed to her effectiveness as a player.

Trinity Rodman

One of the key factors in Trinity's development was her dedication to physical conditioning. Recognizing that soccer is a demanding sport that requires both strength and endurance, she invested time and effort into her fitness regimen. Trinity's physical training included strength exercises, cardiovascular workouts, and agility drills. Her commitment to maintaining peak physical condition allowed her to compete at a high level and endure the rigors of a professional season.

Trinity also placed a strong emphasis on mental preparation and resilience. Soccer is as much a mental game as it is a physical one, and Trinity understood the importance of mental toughness in performing consistently. She worked on building her confidence, managing pressure, and staying focused during matches. By developing a strong mental game, Trinity was able to maintain her composure in high-stress situations and recover from setbacks with resilience.

Coaching played a significant role in shaping Trinity's style and skills. Throughout her career, she worked with various coaches who provided guidance and feedback on her performance. These coaches helped her identify areas for improvement and provided tailored training programs to address specific aspects of her game. Their insights and expertise were instrumental in Trinity's growth as a player, and she valued their contributions to her development.

In addition to formal coaching, Trinity also sought opportunities to learn from experienced players and mentors. By observing and interacting with established professionals, she gained valuable insights into the nuances of the game. These interactions allowed her to learn from others' experiences and incorporate new techniques and strategies into her own play.

Trinity's development was also influenced by her experiences playing in different leagues and competitions. Each level of play presented its own challenges and opportunities for growth. From youth leagues to college soccer and eventually the professional ranks, Trinity faced diverse opponents and scenarios that helped her refine her skills. Competing against different styles of play and adapting to various levels of competition contributed to her overall development as a player.

Trinity Rodman

One of the defining characteristics of Trinity's playing style is her creativity and flair. She is known for her ability to execute dazzling moves and unpredictable plays that catch defenders off guard. This creativity is a result of her willingness to take risks and experiment with different approaches on the field. Trinity's flair for the dramatic adds an exciting element to her play and makes her a fan favorite.

Throughout her career, Trinity has continued to evolve and adapt her style to meet the demands of the game. As she gains more experience and matures as a player, she has refined her approach and expanded her repertoire of skills. Her ability to balance technical proficiency with tactical awareness has allowed her to excel in various roles and positions on the field.

One notable aspect of Trinity's development is her commitment to continuous improvement. She approaches each season with a mindset of learning and growing, always seeking ways to enhance her performance. Whether it's through individual practice sessions, team training, or feedback from coaches, Trinity remains dedicated to pushing her limits and striving for excellence.

Her development has also been influenced by her involvement in high-level competitions and international play. Competing on the global stage has exposed her to diverse playing styles and strategies, further enriching her understanding of the game. Trinity's experiences in international tournaments have broadened her perspective and contributed to her overall growth as a player.

Trinity's development has not only been about refining her skills but also about embracing her unique playing style. She has developed a signature approach that combines technical prowess with a dynamic and creative flair. Her ability to blend skill with individuality makes her a distinctive and impactful player in the world of soccer.

Trinity Rodman's development of her style and skills has been a multifaceted journey characterized by dedication, hard work, and a commitment to excellence. From her early days as a youth player to her current status as a top professional, Trinity's evolution on the field has been marked by continuous improvement and a relentless pursuit of greatness. Her distinctive playing style, combined with her technical and tactical abilities, has solidified her reputation as one of the most exciting talents in women's soccer.

• CHAPTER 10: INTERNATIONAL RECOGNITION AND SUCCESS

Trinity Rodman's journey in soccer has been marked by a series of achievements that have earned her significant international recognition and acclaim. Her rapid rise in the world of women's soccer is a testament to her exceptional talent, hard work, and the impact she has had on the sport on a global scale. This section delves into the key milestones that have cemented Trinity's status as a prominent figure in international soccer.

Trinity Rodman's entry onto the international stage was highlighted by her selection to represent the United States in the U.S. Women's National Team (USWNT). Her exceptional performances in the National Women's Soccer League (NWSL) drew the attention of national team selectors, and she earned her debut in 2021. Being called up to play for the USWNT was a significant milestone in her career, marking her transition from a promising young talent to a recognized international player.

Her debut for the national team was not only a personal achievement but also a recognition of her potential to contribute to the team's success. Trinity's inclusion in the squad was a testament to her skill, athleticism, and the impact she had made in the NWSL. Her performances in her initial appearances showcased her ability to perform on a global stage and highlighted her potential to become a key player for the USWNT.

One of the notable achievements in Trinity's international career came with her participation in the SheBelieves Cup. The SheBelieves Cup is a prestigious international tournament featuring some of the best national teams from around the world. Trinity's inclusion in the tournament provided her with the opportunity to compete against top-level competition and demonstrate her abilities on an international stage. Her performances in the SheBelieves Cup were marked by impressive contributions and solidified her reputation as a rising star in women's soccer.

Trinity's success in international tournaments was further underscored by her participation in the Tokyo 2020 Olympic Games. The Olympics are one of the most prestigious events in sports, and Trinity's selection to represent the USWNT in Tokyo was a significant achievement. Competing in the Olympics allowed Trinity to showcase her talents on a global platform and compete against some of the best players from around the world.

During the Tokyo Olympics, Trinity made a notable impact with her performances. Her contributions were instrumental in helping the USWNT advance through the tournament and compete at the highest level. The experience of competing in the Olympics was a valuable one for Trinity, providing her with exposure to different playing styles and a deeper understanding of international soccer dynamics.

Another major international success for Trinity Rodman came with her recognition in global soccer awards and honors. Her performances in domestic and international competitions did not go unnoticed, and she received several accolades that highlighted her achievements. These awards recognized not only her individual talent but also her contributions to the success of her teams.

Trinity Rodman

Trinity's success on the international stage has also been reflected in her growing global fan base and media presence. As her profile has risen, she has become a prominent figure in the media, with features and interviews showcasing her journey and achievements. Her growing visibility has helped raise awareness of women's soccer and contributed to the sport's global popularity.

In addition to her achievements with the USWNT, Trinity Rodman has been involved in various international club competitions. Her participation in these competitions allowed her to gain valuable experience and compete against top clubs from different countries. These experiences have further enriched her understanding of the game and contributed to her development as a player.

Trinity's impact extends beyond her on-field performances. She has used her platform to advocate for important issues in soccer and beyond. Her involvement in promoting diversity and inclusion within the sport has been a significant aspect of her international recognition. Trinity's commitment to using her voice to address important social issues has resonated with fans and further solidified her status as a role model and ambassador for the sport.

The recognition and success that Trinity Rodman has achieved internationally are a reflection of her dedication, skill, and perseverance. Her journey from a young talent to a globally recognized player is a testament to her hard work and the support of those around her. Trinity's accomplishments on the international stage have not only elevated her own profile but have also contributed to the growth and popularity of women's soccer.

As Trinity continues to develop and excel in her career, her international success is likely to grow even further. Her talent, combined with her determination and commitment to the game, positions her as one of the leading figures in women's soccer. The impact she has made on the international stage is a testament to her abilities and the significant role she plays in the sport's global landscape.

Trinity Rodman's international recognition and success are a testament to her exceptional talent and hard work. From her debut with the USWNT to her participation in major international tournaments and global awards, Trinity's achievements have solidified her status as a prominent figure in women's soccer. Her impact on the sport extends beyond her performances on the field, as she continues to use her platform to advocate for important issues and inspire others. Trinity's journey and accomplishments are a reflection of her dedication to the sport and her significant contributions to the global soccer community.

• CHAPTER 11: IMPACT ON WOMEN'S SOCCER

Trinity Rodman's influence on women's soccer has been profound, marked by her exceptional talent, distinctive style of play, and advocacy for the sport. Her journey from a promising young athlete to a leading figure in the world of soccer has not only garnered individual accolades but has also contributed significantly to the growth and visibility of women's soccer on a global scale. This section explores the various ways in which Trinity Rodman has made an impact on the sport, both on and off the field.

From the outset of her professional career, Trinity Rodman has demonstrated an extraordinary level of skill and athleticism. Her playing style, characterized by dynamic dribbling, precise passing, and powerful shooting, has set her apart as one of the most exciting talents in women's soccer. Trinity's ability to create scoring opportunities and execute intricate plays has made her a standout player in the National Women's Soccer League (NWSL) and on the international stage. Her performances have not only delighted fans but have also elevated the level of play within the league.

One of the significant ways Trinity has impacted women's soccer is through her role in increasing the visibility of the sport. As one of the top young talents in the game, Trinity has attracted considerable attention from media, fans, and sponsors. Her presence in the NWSL and her performances for the U.S. Women's National Team (USWNT) have helped to bring greater focus to women's soccer. This increased visibility has been crucial in promoting the sport and encouraging greater investment and interest in women's soccer at both the professional and grassroots levels.

Trinity's impact extends beyond her on-field performances. She has become a prominent advocate for the advancement of women's soccer and gender equality in sports. Her platform has allowed her to speak out on important issues related to women's sports, including the need for increased support, better opportunities, and fair treatment for female athletes. Trinity's advocacy has helped to raise awareness about the challenges faced by women in soccer and has contributed to ongoing efforts to address these issues.

Her involvement in promoting women's soccer is also reflected in her engagement with youth and grassroots programs. Trinity has used her profile to inspire young players and encourage their participation in the sport. By sharing her experiences and successes, she serves as a role model for aspiring athletes and helps to foster a new generation of soccer players. Her efforts in this area are crucial in ensuring the continued growth and development of women's soccer at the youth level.

Trinity Rodman's influence on the sport is also evident in the way she has redefined the expectations of female athletes. Her exceptional skill set and professional approach to the game have set a new standard for what is possible in women's soccer. Trinity's success has demonstrated that female athletes can achieve the highest levels of performance and recognition, challenging traditional perceptions and paving the way for future generations of female soccer players.

Trinity Rodman

Another significant aspect of Trinity's impact is her role in breaking barriers and expanding opportunities for women in soccer. Her achievements have helped to challenge stereotypes and open doors for other female athletes. By excelling in a highly competitive environment and achieving success on both domestic and international stages, Trinity has helped to demonstrate that women can compete at the highest levels of the sport.

Her participation in major international tournaments, such as the SheBelieves Cup and the Olympic Games, has further highlighted her impact on women's soccer. Competing against top teams from around the world, Trinity has showcased her talent on a global stage and contributed to the success of the USWNT. Her performances in these high-profile events have garnered widespread attention and have reinforced the importance of women's soccer in the international sporting landscape.

Trinity's influence extends to her role as a brand ambassador and public figure. Her presence in the media and her interactions with fans have helped to promote women's soccer and increase its profile.

Trinity Rodman

Through interviews, social media, and public appearances, Trinity has been able to connect with a broad audience and generate interest in the sport. Her ability to engage with fans and communicate the excitement of soccer has contributed to the growing popularity of women's soccer.

The impact of Trinity Rodman on women's soccer is also reflected in the way she has contributed to the development of the game's tactical and technical aspects. Her innovative style of play and her approach to the game have influenced coaches and players alike. By showcasing new techniques and strategies, Trinity has helped to expand the understanding of women's soccer and has contributed to the evolution of the game.

Trinity's achievements and success have also had a positive effect on the growth of the NWSL. Her performances have attracted attention to the league and have helped to elevate its status within the soccer community. As one of the league's standout players, Trinity has played a key role in increasing the league's profile and demonstrating the high level of talent present in women's professional soccer.

Trinity Rodman

Furthermore, Trinity's impact on women's soccer is evident in the way she has contributed to the broader conversation about female athletes and their contributions to sport. Her success has helped to highlight the importance of supporting women's sports and recognizing the achievements of female athletes. Trinity's advocacy and visibility have been instrumental in driving conversations about gender equality and the need for greater investment in women's sports.

Trinity Rodman's impact on women's soccer has been substantial and multifaceted. From her exceptional performances on the field to her advocacy for the sport and her role as a role model, Trinity has made significant contributions to the growth and visibility of women's soccer. Her achievements have not only elevated her own profile but have also helped to advance the sport as a whole. As Trinity continues to excel in her career, her influence on women's soccer is likely to grow even further, inspiring future generations of players and contributing to the ongoing development of the game.

• CHAPTER 12: THE FUTURE OF A RISING SOCCER STAR

Trinity Rodman stands on the precipice of a remarkable future in soccer, poised to continue her rise as one of the sport's most dynamic and influential figures. As a young athlete with already impressive achievements and a growing reputation, the trajectory of her career suggests a future filled with potential and promise. This section explores the various dimensions of Trinity Rodman's future in soccer, including her continued development, potential milestones, and the broader impact she may have on the sport.

Trinity's ongoing development as a player is a critical aspect of her future. Her dedication to improving her skills, understanding the game, and adapting to new challenges will play a significant role in shaping her career. As she gains more experience and matures both physically and mentally, Trinity is likely to refine her techniques and expand her tactical knowledge. Her commitment to continuous improvement suggests that she will continue to evolve as a player, potentially reaching new heights in her performance and contributions on the field.

One of the key areas of focus for Trinity's future is her potential to achieve even greater success in domestic and international competitions. As a standout player in the National Women's Soccer League (NWSL) and a member of the U.S. Women's National Team (USWNT), Trinity is well-positioned to make significant impacts in upcoming tournaments and leagues. Her continued success in these arenas could lead to further accolades and recognition, solidifying her status as one of the top players in the sport.

Trinity's future prospects also include the potential for participation in major international events, such as the FIFA Women's World Cup and the Olympic Games. These tournaments represent some of the highest levels of competition in women's soccer and offer opportunities for players to showcase their talents on a global stage. Trinity's past performances and her potential for future growth suggest that she could be a key player in these prestigious events, contributing to her team's success and gaining further recognition.

Trinity Rodman

Another aspect of Trinity's future involves her influence on the growth and development of women's soccer. As a prominent figure in the sport, she has the potential to inspire and impact aspiring young players. Her achievements and the visibility she brings to women's soccer can help drive interest in the sport, encourage more young athletes to participate, and contribute to the overall growth of the game. Trinity's role as a role model and ambassador for women's soccer will likely continue to be an important aspect of her career.

In addition to her contributions on the field, Trinity's future may also involve expanding her impact off the field. Her involvement in advocacy for women's sports and gender equality has already made a significant difference, and she may continue to use her platform to address important issues. Whether through public speaking, community engagement, or involvement in charitable initiatives, Trinity's influence extends beyond her performances and can contribute to positive changes in the sport and society.

Trinity Rodman

Trinity's potential future achievements are also linked to her ability to adapt to evolving trends and developments in soccer. As the sport continues to grow and change, players must stay abreast of new strategies, technologies, and playing styles. Trinity's willingness to embrace innovation and her openness to learning will be important factors in her continued success. Her ability to stay ahead of trends and adapt her game to new challenges will contribute to her long-term success in soccer.

The potential for Trinity to achieve milestones such as breaking records or setting new standards in women's soccer is also a significant aspect of her future. As she continues to develop her skills and gain experience, she may have opportunities to achieve notable individual and team accomplishments. Whether through setting new records, winning major awards, or leading her teams to victory in important tournaments, Trinity's future in soccer holds the potential for remarkable achievements.

Trinity's future career trajectory may also involve opportunities for growth and development in various aspects of her professional life. This could include potential moves to different teams or leagues, collaborations with sponsors and brands, and involvement in soccer-related projects and initiatives. As her profile continues to rise, Trinity may have opportunities to explore new avenues within the sport and beyond, contributing to her overall growth as an athlete and a public figure.

Another important aspect of Trinity's future is her continued engagement with her fans and the soccer community. Building and maintaining strong relationships with supporters, engaging with fans through social media, and participating in community events will be key to her ongoing success and influence. Trinity's ability to connect with her audience and contribute to the broader soccer community will play a role in shaping her future and ensuring her continued popularity and impact.

As Trinity Rodman looks ahead to her future in soccer, her focus on maintaining peak physical and mental condition will be crucial. The demands of professional soccer require players to stay in top form, both physically and mentally. Trinity's commitment to her fitness, nutrition, and mental preparation will play a significant role in her ability to perform at the highest level and achieve her future goals.

Trinity Rodman's future in soccer is marked by significant potential and promise. With her ongoing development, potential for major achievements, and impact both on and off the field, Trinity is well-positioned to continue her rise as one of the sport's leading figures. Her dedication to improvement, advocacy for women's sports, and ability to adapt to new challenges will contribute to her future success and influence. As Trinity's career progresses, her contributions to soccer and her impact on the sport's growth and development will continue to be significant, shaping the future of women's soccer and inspiring the next generation of players.

• CONCLUSION

Trinity Rodman's journey in women's soccer is a compelling narrative of talent, determination, and ambition. From her early years as a promising athlete to her rise as a leading figure in the sport, Trinity's career has been characterized by significant achievements and a relentless drive to excel. Her story is not just one of personal success but also a testament to the evolving landscape of women's soccer and the broader impact of her contributions.

Trinity's rise in the soccer world has been nothing short of remarkable. Her exceptional performances in the National Women's Soccer League (NWSL) and with the U.S. Women's National Team (USWNT) have established her as one of the sport's most exciting and influential players. Her skill, athleticism, and dedication have not only earned her numerous accolades but have also captivated fans and inspired young athletes around the world. Trinity's ability to make an impact on the field is a reflection of her hard work and passion for the game.

Trinity Rodman

Beyond her on-field achievements, Trinity Rodman's influence extends to her role as a role model and advocate for women's soccer. Her efforts to promote the sport, address important issues, and inspire the next generation of players have been integral to her success. Trinity's commitment to using her platform to advocate for gender equality and the growth of women's soccer demonstrates her dedication to making a positive difference both within and outside of the sport.

As Trinity's career continues to evolve, her future in soccer holds immense potential. Her ongoing development as a player, her contributions to major international tournaments, and her ability to inspire and engage with fans all point to a future filled with possibilities. Trinity's trajectory suggests that she will continue to achieve remarkable milestones and contribute significantly to the growth and popularity of women's soccer.

In reflecting on Trinity Rodman's journey, it is clear that her impact on the sport is profound and multifaceted. From her early beginnings to her current status as a rising star, Trinity's story highlights the progress and potential of women's soccer. Her achievements are a testament to her talent and perseverance, while her advocacy and influence underscore her commitment to advancing the sport.

Trinity Rodman's biography is not just a chronicle of her career but a celebration of the transformative role she plays in women's soccer. As she continues to make strides in the sport, her legacy will undoubtedly inspire future generations of players and contribute to the ongoing development of women's soccer. Her story serves as a powerful reminder of the possibilities that arise when talent, hard work, and dedication come together to shape a remarkable career.

Made in the USA
Monee, IL
05 April 2025

15232105R00056